FREESTYLE
SOCCER
TRICKS

Acknowledgments

I owe a huge debt to two people in particular: my late father, Frankie, who thought all the tricks I did with a ball were fantastic, and believed in me and what I wanted to do; and my wife, Ethel, who thinks all the tricks I do look exactly the same, but still believes in me and what I do. Without their support and understanding over the years, I would surely have given up.

A big "thank you" must go out to all the players and freestylers who have given me ideas or shown me new tricks over the last 20 years. I have been very fortunate that many people have been kind enough to help me become a better freestyler, and hopefully this book will help many others.

Keep practicing.

Sean

FREESTYLE SOCCER TRICKS

tricks

flick-ups

catches

Sean D'Arcy

FIREFLY BOOKS

A FIREFLY BOOK

Published by Firefly Books Ltd. 2008

Copyright © 2008 Sean D'Arcy
Cover photograph © 2008 April Ward
Inside photogr aphs © 2008 April Ward, except Pvi,
courtesy of the author, and Pviii © 2008 Getty Images

Second printing, 2010

Publisher Cataloging-in-Publication Data (U.S.)

D'Arcy, Sean.
    Freestyle soccer tricks : tricks, flick-ups, catches /
Sean D'Arcy.
[120] p. : col. photos. ; cm.
Summary: Learn how to perform top soccer tricks from
a professional freestyler. Each trick is outlined step by
step, and includes variations, tips and how to
overcome any difficulties.
ISBN-13: 978-1-55407-404-4 (pbk.)
ISBN-10: 1-55407-404-5 (pbk.)
    1. Soccer. I. Title.
796.334 dc22   G V943.D3373   2008

**Library and Archives Canada Cataloguing in
Publication**

D'Arcy, Sean
    Freestyle soccer tricks : tricks, flick-ups, catches /
Sean D'Arcy.
ISBN-13: 978-1-55407-404-4 (pbk.)
ISBN-10: 1-55407-404-5 (pbk.)
    1. Soccer. I. Title.
GV943.D27 2008   796.334   C2008-901079-5

Published in the United States by
Firefly Books (U.S.) Inc.
P.O. Box 1338, Ellicott Station
Buffalo, New York 14205

Published in Canada by
Firefly Books Ltd.
66 Leek Crescent
Richmond Hill, Ontario L4B 1H1

First published 2007 by
A&C Black Publishers Ltd
38 Soho Square, London W1D 3HB
www.acblack.com

Cover design by Jocelyn Lucas
Text design and typesetting by James Watson

Printed and bound in China

Note: It is always the responsibility of the individual to
assess his or her own fitness capability before
participating in any training activity. Whilst every effort
has been made to ensure the content of this book is as
technically accurate as possible, neither the author nor
the publishers can accept r esponsibility for any injury
or loss sustained as a result of the use of this material.

CONTENTS

Introduction

Hello, my name is Sean D'Arcy and I'm a professional soccer freestyler. I travel all over the world doing demonstrations and teaching players how to do tricks. I'm going to show you how to do the amazing juggling tricks you see the world's best soccer players doing. Learning the tricks will improve your coordination, balance and ball control, and make you more confident using your weaker foot when you play soccer.

I've always loved freestyle, and when I had to give up playing soccer because of illness I became a freestyler because I couldn't imagine my life without kicking a ball in some way. I practiced and practiced and worked really hard, and so now, although I'm not a professional player, I feel I'm almost living my dream because soccer is still such a big part of my life.

First, there is a chapter 1 with exercises and then chapter 2 with juggling drills to get you started. I've divided the tricks themselves into three different chapters. Chapter 3 shows you flick-ups. This is when the ball is on the ground and you use your feet to get it up into the air. You can do all of the flick-up tricks before you learn to juggle a ball. Chapter 4 is about catches and I'll show you a way to practice the catch from your hands so, again, you can do all these tricks before you learn to juggle. Chapter 5 is all about juggling tricks and you'll need to be able to juggle a ball to do them.

I've had a fantastic time writing this book and I know you'll enjoy learning all the tricks. If you need any more tips or advice, check out my website at www.footballtricks.com.

Learning How to Juggle

I'm going to give you some exercises first, and you need to be patient and do each exercise five times with each foot. It should take only a few minutes to do them all and soon you'll be able to juggle!

Tip

Juggle near a wall (without windows!) so that if you lose control the ball bounces back to you. Or juggle on grass so the ball doesn't roll as far as it would on a hard surface like a road.

1 Hold the ball in your hands and gently drop it onto your foot. Then kick it back up and catch it with your hands.

2 Drop the ball and let it bounce once, then kick it back up into your hands.

3 Drop the ball and let it bounce once, then kick up with your stronger foot. Let it bounce once more, then kick it with your weaker foot back up into your hands.

Once you're confident with those exercises, you're ready to move on to using your knees.

4 Hold the ball up a bit higher than before and gently drop it. Lift your knee up, let the ball bounce off your knee and catch it again in your hands.

5 Drop the ball gently and lift up your knee so the ball will bounce up off it. Then let the ball bounce once on the ground, kick it back up with your foot and catch it in your hands.

6 Drop the ball gently again and let it bounce on the ground. Kick it up once with your foot, then do one bounce off your knee up into your hands.

Now that you're feeling confident, this is the time to go for your personal best and set your record for how many times you can kick the ball up with only one bounce in between each kick.

OK – now it's time to try some of the harder exercises...

7 Drop the ball, bounce it off one knee, then kick it back up into your hands.

8 Drop the ball and kick it up with your stronger foot, then kick it with your weaker foot back into your hands.

9 Drop the ball and do two kicks with your stronger foot, then one bounce on the ground, and then two kicks with your weaker foot and catch.

After all that hard work it's time to have some fun!

10 Standing up, drop the ball and let it bounce, then slap it back down as hard as you can with the bottom of your foot so that it bounces up high and you can catch it.

Now let's play a game. I want you to try to get up to the highest number of kicks you can by first doing one kick then letting the ball bounce, then keeping the ball off the ground for two kicks before letting it bounce, then three, then four and so on. Just to make it more difficult, if you mess up you have to go back to the beginning with one kick and a bounce.

Doing these simple exercises I bet you've had a couple of hundred kicks in less than 10 minutes. That's a lot more than you would have had if you'd gone for a new record each time. Taking it slowly really does make learning to juggle easier.

SECRETS OF JUGGLING

Outside of your foot

If you're having trouble using the outside of your foot then it's normally because of one of two problems:

To kick the ball properly, your whole foot needs to be level to the ground. If the ball goes out in front of you, you're probably lifting your heel with your toe still pointing downward. This means your foot is on a slope, so when you hit the ball it bounces off at an angle rather than heading back up.

If the ball goes sideways, this could be because you haven't lifted your foot up high enough. When you kick the ball, your foot should be at about the same height as your hip. This problem happens if you try to kick the ball when it's too close to your body. You need a bit more room, so a little step away from the ball first will help.

Shoulders

If you have your arms outstretched when you juggle with your shoulders, the ball will go all over the place.

Here's the secret: the ball will go in the opposite direction to the way your elbows are pointing. So if your arms are tucked in by your side with your elbows pointing straight down, the ball will go straight up. But if you have your arms outstretched, your elbows are pointing away from your body and the ball will go over your head.

Another excellent tip is to remember to move your feet to make sure you hit the ball in the middle of your shoulder. So you need to adjust your position with lots of small, quick steps.

Tip

Watch where the ball goes when you make a mistake. The ball will only go the way you kicked it, so think what could have caused that to happen.

Head

First, don't jump at the ball. Instead, you need to use your knees to bounce up and down as you head the ball. Use your forehead, and keep your eyes open so you can see where the ball is going.

If, when you head the ball, it always goes in front of you, you need to tilt your head back a little bit more. If the ball always goes behind you, your head is tilted back too far. If the ball goes sideways, you need to move your feet a bit more to make sure that you are right under the ball.

It's hard juggling a ball with your head more than a few times in a row. Again, the best advice I can give you is to take it slowly until you've got the technique right. Use the one-header-then-one-catch method, just like we used with our feet.

Chest

Chest bounces look awesome, but the good news is that they aren't that difficult to perform. Just like heading, the main thing to remember is not to jump at the ball. Instead, use your knees to bounce up and chest the ball upward. Lean back so that your chest is level with the ground and bend your knees to bring your upper body up and down.

If you find the ball is going forward, it's because you're not leaning back far enough. If the ball seems to stick to your chest and not bounce very high, it's because you haven't bounced with your knees, so your chest has not come up to hit the ball. If the ball goes over your head off your chest, this is because you're leaning back too much.

Now that you've learned these secrets, it's time to have a go at some drills!

Juggling Drills

Juggling drills are harder because you have to kick the ball in an organized pattern. It's a terrific way to really work on your ball control. One huge benefit is that you'll find that your weaker foot or leg will get much stronger and you'll become more confident using it when you play a real game of soccer.

When you're doing these drills, you really have to test yourself. Set a target for how many you'll do in a row and increase the target each time. It's the only way to get better.

To make writing out the drills less complicated, I'll use abbreviations for the different parts of the body and whether it's on your stronger or weaker side:

T TOP OF FOOT (WHERE THE LACES ARE ON YOUR SHOES)
I INSIDE OF FOOT
O OUTSIDE OF FOOT
K KNEE
SH SHOULDER
H HEAD
CH CHEST
ß BACK
(S) STRONGER FOOT
(W) WEAKER FOOT
⋰ NEXT TOUCH

The Box

This is a fabulous and simple way of finding out if you can control the ball with your weaker foot.

It goes like this:

T(S) ⫶ K(S) ⫶ K(W) ⫶ T(W)

Variation

You could do the Box the other way around, starting with your weaker foot, but an even better variation is to go across the Box each time like this:

T(S) ⫶ K(W) ⫶ T(W) ⫶ K(S)

The fantastic 5

This has been variously called the Pele 5, Keegan 5 and Beckham 5.

It goes like this:

T(S) ⋗ K(S) ⋗ H ⋗ K(W) ⋗ T(W)

Variation

A "fantastic" variation is to go across your body like this:

T(S) ⋗ K(W) ⋗ H ⋗ K(S) ⋗ T(W)

Super 7

Of all the drills I'm asked to do, this is
the one that's requested the most. It's
also called the Maradona 7.

It goes like this:

**T(S) ⸽ K(S) ⸽ SH(S) ⸽ H ⸽ SH(W) ⸽
K(W) ⸽ T(W)**

Variation

A "super" variation is to go across your
body:

**T(W) ⸽ T(S) ⸽ K(W) ⸽ K(S) ⸽ SH(W) ⸽
SH(S) ⸽ H**

Super 7 Plus 2

I get a much better reaction when I do a Super 8 and a Super 9, as players can't guess what the extra touches are going to be.

SUPER 8

T(W) ⫶ T(S) ⫶ K(W) ⫶ K(S) ⫶ CH ⫶ SH(W) ⫶ SH(S) ⫶ H

SUPER 9

T(W) ⫶ T(S) ⫶ K(W) ⫶ K(S) ⫶ CH ⫶ SH(W) ⫶ SH(S) ⫶ H ⫶ B

Tip

You really have to bend your knees and hit the ball hard off your chest to get it high enough to go to your shoulder.

Around the Clock

Definitely the ultimate juggling drill and one that will impress everyone when they see you doing it!

It goes like this:

T(S) ⋗ **I (S)** ⋗ **O(S)** ⋗ **K(S)** ⋗ **SH(S)** ⋗ **H** ⋗ **SH(W)** ⋗ **K(W)** ⋗ **O(W)** ⋗ **I(W)** ⋗ **T(W)**

Variation

Introduce a chest bounce that doesn't make it any harder but makes it look sensational:

T(S) ⋗ **I (S)** ⋗ **O(S)** ⋗ **K(S)** ⋗ **CH** ⋗ **SH(S)** ⋗ **H** ⋗ **SH(W)** ⋗ **K(W)** ⋗ **O(W)** ⋗ **I(W)** ⋗ **T(W)**

Tip

As you'd expect with the ultimate juggling drill, this one isn't easy. But it isn't impossible either. I want you to think about *when* you're going to do it, not *whether* you are going to do it.

The Specs

People often ask me why I call this drill the Specs – to me it looks as if the ball draws two big circles like a pair of spectacles!

T(S) ⟫ I(S) ⟫ K(S) ⟫ O(S) ⟫ T(S) ⟫
T(W) ⟫ I(W) ⟫ K(W) ⟫ O(W) ⟫ T(W)

Variation

A great variation is to go around the other way. I find this way a bit harder but you may find it easier:

T(S) ⟫ O(S) ⟫ K(S) ⟫ I(S) ⟫ T(S) ⟫
T(W) ⟫ O(W) ⟫ K(W) ⟫ I(W) ⟫ T(W)

JUGGLING GAMES

All these games are terrific fun to play and they benefit you when you play real soccer too. When I play any of these games, I set myself a goal of how many points I want before I start and then don't stop till I reach that goal.

5 & Up

This is a brilliant way to practice controlling the ball when it comes down from a height. Simply juggle the ball from foot to foot (not your head!) and on every fifth touch kick the ball above head height.

Variation

A very challenging variation is that every fifth kick has to go over your head. This means you have to turn around and control the ball facing the other way.

Tip

The perfect way to play this game is if you always juggle from one foot to the other, no matter how high the ball goes.

1, 2, 3 and On

All you have to do is one kick with your stronger foot and then one with your weaker foot, then two kicks with your stronger foot and two with your weaker foot, then three, and keep going for one more kick each time.

Variation

Aim for a specific number, say seven kicks. When you reach this, do six kicks, and so on down until you make it all the way back to one kick.

Tip

When you're new to the game, you can use any part of your leg to control the ball. As you get better, only use your feet.

Hands Down

Juggle the ball and count how many times you can touch the ground with both hands at the same time without dropping the ball.

Variation

Instead of putting your hands down, put one or both knees on the ground, sit down, or do a tuck jump. Or pick up a tennis ball and put it back down (this is hard, but great fun). This way, you can make Hands Down as hard or easy as you like!

Trick Square

This game forces you to look around as well as focus on the ball, just like when you play soccer. Mark out a square with sides about 10 steps apart. Juggle the ball while walking around the square and at every corner do something special like five headers or a juggling trick.

Variation

Instead of making a square, make a random shape so that at each corner you could go in any direction.

Drill Counting

With Drill Counting, the number of kicks is less important than the variety. If we use the Fantastic 5 as the drill, you get one point for kicking the ball with your right foot and one for kicking it with your left and so on for each part of a Fantastic 5. But even if you kick the ball 50 times with your right foot, you'll only get one point until you've touched the ball with all the other parts of a Fantastic 5.

Variation

An excellent variation is to do a juggling trick before you start the drill again. When I first tried Drill Counting, I had to do an Around the Clock with a catch on the back of my neck before I could do the drill again. At the time, that was a tough test for me and I found it very tricky to get more than 20 points.

Jump Over the Moon

Jump Over the Moon works on your quick reactions and foot speed. Don't count how many kicks you do but instead how many times you can jump over the ball while juggling. The ball is allowed to bounce once every jump and the only rule is that both feet must leave the ground when you jump.

Tip

Play on a hard surface so the ball bounces higher.

Variation

Limit how many touches you can have between each jump. A bit like when you played Five & Up, try allowing yourself only five kicks between each jump.

Clap, Clap

This brilliant game helps you get into the habit of not always looking at your feet when you play soccer. Kick the ball up and clap your hands together below the ball then above it before you kick it again.

Variation

Try to clap three times: once below, once above, then once below again. You could even go for four claps: two below and two above!

Tip

Kick the ball up to about eye level. If you go really high, the first clap below is easy but the second one above the ball becomes tricky.

Flick-ups

Even if you can't juggle yet, you can still do a flick-up. The first trick in this chapter, the Glory, was the first trick I ever learned and I'm sure that at the time I wasn't very good at juggling. But I remember how great I felt when I did it properly for the first time!

The Glory

Over the years I've taught this trick to children as young as age 4...

Step 1

Grip the ball between your ankles so tightly you can jump around and the ball doesn't fall out.

Tip

The higher you roll the ball up the inside of your leg in Step 2, the easier the trick is to do.

Step 2

Use your stronger foot to roll the ball up the inside of your leg as high as you can while still holding the ball.

Step 3

Hop up as high as you can on your weaker foot and then flick at the ball. The ball will bounce off your heel up into the air!

Variation

Instead of rolling the ball up the inside of your leg, roll it up the back of your leg and then do Step 3. The ball will go right over your head.

Common Problem

"The ball just seems to stick to my legs and goes nowhere."

This happens when your stronger foot that rolled the ball up your leg in Step 2 actually rolls the ball back down again when you hop. To stop this from happening, remember to keep your knee in the air when you hop.

The Forward Roll

Thierry Henry once used this trick in a game to get the ball in the air before volleying it up and across the goal.

Step 1

Start with the ball on the ground a foot's length in front of your weaker foot, with your stronger foot on top of the ball.

Step 2

Use your stronger foot to quickly roll the ball back so it hits the toes of your other foot.

Tip

In Step 1 make sure both feet are in a nice straight line pointing directly in front of you. This makes it much easier for you to roll the ball straight onto your weaker foot.

Step 3

As the ball hits your toes, give a little hop and the ball pops up ready for you to volley it across the goal like Thierry Henry.

Variation

Instead of rolling the ball back in Step 2, backheel it onto your toes. It becomes so much faster that you don't have to hop in Step 3 because the ball will bounce high enough when it hits your toes.

Common Problem

The ball always shoots off in front of me and doesn't go up.

You're hopping too early and stabbing at the ball with the toe of your weaker foot in Step 3, which makes it go forward and not upward.

The Mo'Gy

This is named after Michael O'Grady, the first guy to successfully do the trick when I taught it for the first time.

Step 1

With the ball on the ground, put the toes of your weaker foot so close under the ball that if you wiggle your toes it will wobble a bit.

Step 2

Swing your stronger foot up as high as you can in front of you and then hop off your weaker foot. The ball will lift up into the air.

Tip

If you've tried lots of times but can't do it, start with your stronger foot as high in the air as you can, then hop with your weaker foot and bang the ball down.

Step 3

Bring your stronger foot down and bang the ball back down into the ground with the sole of your foot.

Variation

Do the entire Mo'Gy with one foot. Put your stronger foot under the ball then lift your knee quickly. Spin your foot above the ball and bang it back down again, super-quickly!

Common Problem

The ball seems to get stuck between my feet.

You're not swinging high enough. The ball is hardly off the ground before you're trying to bang it back down, so it just jams between your feet.

The Bang Down

People always ask whether I can bang the ball down so hard it bounces over my head, and the answer is yes!

Step 1

Grip the ball tightly between your ankles.

Tip

You need to get as much height as you can before you bang the ball down, so the faster and higher you can rip your knee upward, the better chance you have of doing the trick.

Step 2

Rip your stronger knee straight up as high and as fast as you can so that the ball spins up into the air.

Step 3

Bang the ball back down into the ground with the heel of your stronger foot. The ball bounces up.

Variation

In Step 3, instead of banging the ball back down, swing your stronger foot under the ball and begin juggling. It makes you look like you have superhuman foot speed.

Common Problem

I stamp on the ball and it doesn't bounce up.

Your stronger foot must come down at an angle when you hit the ball in Step 3 and it must finish up out in front of you.

The Squeeze

This is a great trick to teach younger players because it's simple and quick to explain and do.

Step 1

Start with the ball between your feet, but not touching them, with the middle of the ball in line with your little toes.

Step 2

Snap your feet together as quickly as you can under the ball. The ball will pop straight up in the air for you to begin juggling.

Tip

The faster you snap your feet together, the higher the ball goes.

Variation

In Step 1, cross your legs over so that the ball is between the outsides of your feet and then do the Squeeze.

Common Problem

The ball always goes off to the side and not straight up.

All you have to do is double-check in Step 1 that both feet are the same distance away from the ball when you begin, so that they snap the ball together.

The Shamrock

An extremely eye-catching way to begin a routine...

Step 1

Squeeze the ball tightly between your ankles, but this time lean forward just a bit.

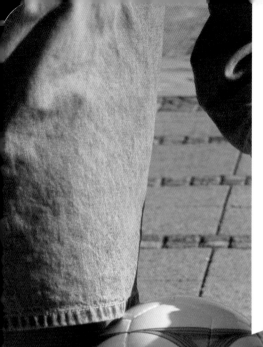

Step 2

Lift your stronger foot up behind you as quickly as you can. The ball will spin up in the air.

Step 3

Slam the ball straight back down into the ground with the laces on your stronger foot. It'll bounce straight up over your head and come down in front of you.

Tip

In lots of tricks Step 2 is important, but in this trick it's vital. You need to get the ball as high as you can, so you really need to lift that stronger foot up quickly.

Common Problem

The ball hits the back of my head.

You're tilting your head back too early to see where the ball is. Wait a bit longer before you look up.

The Spin

Whenever I demonstrate this trick, someone will say they'll never be able to do it – but they always can!

Step 1

Have you guessed it? Yes, grip the ball firmly between your ankles.

Tip

To help you spin in the right direction, hold your weaker hand out behind your back and watch the ball as you spin it up toward your hand, then spin around.

Step 2

Use your stronger foot to rip the ball straight up the back of your weaker leg so that the ball spins upward. The higher the ball goes, the easier it is to do the Spin.

Step 3

Spin on your weaker foot and swing your stronger foot around from behind your leg to the front. The ball will be right there in front of you to begin juggling.

Variation

Cross your stronger leg behind your weaker leg and squeeze the ball between the outside of your weaker leg and the toes of your stronger foot. Rip the ball up the outside of your weaker leg and spin.

Common Problem

I'm doing everything right, but I never reach the ball before it bounces.

You're rolling the ball across your weaker leg and not up it. Try rolling the ball up the back of your leg and then spin and catch it in both hands.

The Brazilian

I call this trick the Brazilian because the first time I ever saw it I was watching a Brazilian league game on TV.

Step 1

I think you know what to do! Grip the ball tightly between your ankles.

Tip

This might make it easier for you as you roll the ball up and across your weaker leg: try going on your tiptoes. The extra height makes it easier.

Step 2

Use your stronger foot to rip the ball up and across the back of your weaker leg so it will spin off up in the air to the side.

Step 3

Using the toes of your stronger foot, stab the ball down into the ground so it will bounce up in front of you.

Variation

Start with the ball between the outside of your weaker foot and the toes of your stronger foot, then rip the ball up the outside of your weaker leg and stab it back down.

Common Problem

The ball never bounces. It just gets stuck between my foot and the ground.

Either you're only ripping the ball across your weaker leg, and not up and across, or it could be that you're forgetting to just quickly stab at the ball.

The Cross

This trick is a beauty! Step 1 can seem a little tricky to get the hang of, but once you start the right way the rest is easy.

Step 1

Start with the ball on the ground in front of your weaker foot, with your stronger foot on top of the ball. Now turn your weaker foot so the inside of your foot is facing the ball.

Tip

In Step 1, start with the ball as far in front of your weaker foot as you can manage while still comfortably balancing with your stronger foot on top.

Step 2

Quickly roll the ball back so it hits the inside of your weaker foot.

Step 3

As you feel the ball hit your foot, give a little hop and the ball will pop up for you to begin freestyling.

Variation

Instead of rolling the ball back in Step 2, backheel the ball onto the inside of your foot. It also looks very different, so people think you can do two different tricks!

Common Problems

My legs just get tangled up.

If you have too small a gap between the ball and your weaker foot in Step 1, your legs seem to get in each other's way when you roll the ball back. All you have to do is make the gap bigger.

The Kick

With this trick, the ball pops straight up in front of you and you can do just about any juggling trick right away or blast the ball as hard as you want at the goal.

Step 1

Start with the ball between your feet, but this time make sure it only touches the inside of your weaker foot.

Step 2

Lift your stronger foot up and turn it inward so your toes are pointing at your other foot.

Step 3

Stab your stronger foot under the center of the ball. This will squeeze the ball up into the air so you can begin juggling.

Variation

In Step 2, just lift your stronger foot out to the side and don't turn it inward, so your toes are pointing at your other foot. Then, in Step 3, just swing the inside of your stronger foot under the ball and squeeze the ball up.

Tip

To make sure the ball goes straight up in Step 3, twist your weaker toes inward to stop the ball going forward.

Heel Pop

My current favorite flick-up... I saw it for the first time on a TV ad.

Step 1

Start with both feet on the ground and the ball just in front of your stronger foot. Then take a big step forward with your weaker foot.

Step 2

Put the toes of your stronger foot on top of the ball. Then, as quickly as you can, roll the ball along the sole of your foot until your toes jab into the ground.

Step 3

The ball slams into your heel and pops up into the air behind you. You spin around to start juggling.

Tip

When you jab your toes into the ground in Step 2, leave your heel off the ground just a bit. This makes the ball pop up higher.

Variation

Instead of spinning around when the ball pops up off your heel, tap the ball forward with the inside of your weaker foot. The ball will just float in front of you and you can begin juggling.

Common Problem

The ball hits the back of my stronger leg.

Take a slightly bigger step forward in Step 1 with your weaker foot. When the ball slams into your heel, your feet should be just about next to each other.

The Olympic

This trick is so called because I was lucky enough to see the Brazilian Olympic team doing it in practice.

Step 1

Put your stronger foot on top of the ball with the outside of your weaker foot as far away from the ball as you can manage without overbalancing.

Step 2

Roll the ball quickly with your stronger foot so that it hits the outside of your weaker foot.

Tip

If you can't leave enough of a gap between the ball and your weaker foot to spin the ball up without overbalancing, try using a smaller ball.

Step 3

When it hits, slice your weaker foot under the ball and it'll spin up into the air for you to begin juggling.

Variation

An outstanding combination is an Olympic and then, without touching the ball, a Scissor trick. It looks brilliant and, if you do your Olympic properly, not that hard at all.

Common Problem

The ball hardly comes up in the air at all.

You're either forgetting to slice under the ball in Step 3, or not slicing hard enough.

The Scoop

This is definitely the most deceptive trick I know. It looks easy but is really quite hard!

Step 1

Begin with your stronger foot in the air behind you. The ball should be on the ground next to your weaker foot, exactly where your stronger foot would be if you were standing up straight.

Step 2

Swing your stronger foot down and smoothly slide it under the ball.

Tip

There's no need to do this quickly. Just aim for a nice steady swing.

Step 3

When your stronger foot goes out to the front, you need to bend your toes back and lift your knee straight up. This will make the ball go upward and not forward.

Variation

A brilliant combination with this is to scoop the ball and catch it on the back of your neck. If you do it smoothly enough, it really is one of the best-looking combinations in freestyle.

Common Problem

The ball just goes up and forward.

You're either forgetting to bend your toes back and lift your knee up in Step 3, swinging your foot so fast that bending your toes back just doesn't stop the ball going forward, or in Step 1 the ball is a bit in front of you instead of next to your weaker foot.

The V

With this stylish trick, everything is done with your stronger foot, and your weaker foot just stops you from falling over while you do it.

Step 1

Start with the ball on your stronger side, just in front and to the side of you, and with your stronger foot on top of it. You should be nice and balanced in this position.

Step 2

Drag the ball back past the inside of
your weaker foot so that it rolls behind
your weaker leg.

Tip

When you drag the ball in Step 2, you
don't have to do it quickly. The ball
just needs to be moving.

Step 3

As the ball passes behind your weaker leg, use the big toe of your stronger foot to hook the ball upward and forward to the other side of your weaker leg.

Variation

In Step 3, when you've hooked the ball in the air, spin around on your weaker foot and begin juggling facing in the other direction. It makes it look even more stylish.

Common Problem

The ball keeps hitting the back of my weaker leg.

Make sure the ball is in the right place in Step 1, as you need to drag the ball back at an angle before you hook it up from behind your leg.

The Side Roll

This is one of those tricks that you either find really easy or really hard, so stick to it if you don't succeed first time.

Step 1

Start with both feet on the ground. The ball should be just a little bit to your stronger side, with your stronger foot on top of it.

Step 2

Roll the ball as fast as you can so that the ball hits the inside of your weaker foot.

Step 3

Swing your stronger foot under the ball when it bounces up off the inside of your weaker foot.

Variation

In Step 2, instead of rolling the ball with the sole of your foot, backheel it onto the inside of your foot. To avoid jamming the ball between your heel and the inside of your weaker foot, try to swing your stronger foot so that it finishes behind your weaker leg and out of the way. This will allow the ball to bounce up.

Tip

The whole trick depends on how fast you roll the ball in Step 2. If it isn't fast enough, the trick won't work, even if everything else is right.

Common Problem

The ball doesn't go up high enough to start juggling.

You're not rolling the ball quickly enough. To get a bit more speed, start with the ball out further to your side in Step 1.

Catches

With all the catches in this chapter, I've described a way you can practice from your hands, so even if you can't juggle at all you can still learn these tricks.

Foot Catch

Suddenly catching a fast-moving ball on your foot is a very impressive trick.

THE HOLD

The ball is squeezed between your toes and your shin. The best way to get familiar with how it feels is to do this:

1. Start with your foot flat on the ground with the ball just in front of it.

2. Put your hand on top of the ball and roll the ball slowly up your foot till it touches your shin.

3. When the ball touches your shin, bend your toes up till they touch the ball.

4. Lift your foot off the ground and move it up and down a few times. If the ball doesn't fall out, you're halfway there already to catching it.

THE TRICK
Step 1

Start with the ball in your hands. Gently throw the ball straight up as you lift your stronger knee up.

Step 2

Move your stronger foot so that when the ball falls back down it'll hit your foot.

Tip

Spin the ball slightly back toward you when you throw it up. The higher you throw the ball, the harder it is to catch, so don't go above head height.

Step 3

When the ball is about to hit your stronger foot, begin to lower it and bring your toes up into the hold position. The ball will be gently caught as your foot goes down.

Common Problem

I'm bringing my foot down, but the ball just bounces off.

You are bringing your foot down way too early, probably as soon as the ball starts to drop. This means your foot is already on the ground before the ball hits.

Back of the Neck Catch

This is definitely the world's best-known juggling trick.

THE HOLD

You hold the ball on the back of your neck with four parts of your body. The back of your head will stop the ball going forward, your elbows will stop it rolling off the sides and the middle of your back stops it rolling backward.

1 Bend in the middle so that you're looking down at the ground.

2 While only moving your head, look straight ahead in front of you.

3 Lift your elbows up so they're higher than your back.

THE TRICK
Step 1

Start with the ball in your hands. Throw it just above head height so that, if you don't move, the ball will drop straight back into your hands.

Step 2

Keep watching the ball all the time. Just as it is coming down to about the height of your head, drop into the hold so that the ball will hit the back of your neck.

Tip

Do everything smoothly. Don't fling your elbows up or drop down really quickly. The more smoothly you move, the more likely you are to catch the ball.

Step 3

When the ball touches the back of your neck, bend your knees. This way you'll cushion the impact and the ball will nestle gently into the hold.

Variation

You still catch the ball on the back of your neck, but in the push-up position. This time your elbows bend to cushion the impact and not your knees. Tricky, but fun!

Common Problem

The ball always rolls off and bounces on the ground in front of me.

When you're bending over, you're forgetting to keep your head up. Try to look at something in the distance like goalposts at the other end of a field.

Leg Jam

To do this catch properly the ball has to grip onto the back of your leg. A new ball is very smooth and won't grip, so try using an older ball.

THE HOLD

The ball is held between your calf, your heel and the back of your leg:

1 Use your hand to press the ball into the spot where the cheek of your bottom and your leg meet.

2 Lift your heel up and press the ball into that spot. This is the perfect position to catch the ball. To make sure you have the hold right, you should be able to hop around a bit without dropping the ball.

THE TRICK
Step 1

Start with the ball in your hands at about waist height. Spin the ball up in the air so that it will bounce about 3–6 feet (1–2 m) in front of you and with enough spin so that, if you didn't move, it would bounce straight back into your hands.

Tip

As well as using an older, grippier ball, let some air out – but not too much, as the ball still has to be able to bounce back in Step 1.

Step 2

While the ball is still in the air, turn 180 degrees and position yourself so that when the ball bounces back it'll hit the back of your stronger leg in the spot described in the hold.

Step 3

When the ball hits that spot, smoothly bring your heel up to gently press the ball against the back of your leg.

Variation

Simply do everything in reverse: instead of catching the ball with your heel, catch it with the back of your leg. Put your knee and toes on the ground with your heel pointing up. When the ball lands on your heel, place the back of your leg on top of the ball to hold it there.

Common Problem

The ball bangs off my heel and almost hits me in the face.

You have to be patient and wait for the ball! You're bringing your heel up too early.

The Shinny

I can honestly say that I did this trick the first time I tried it and I've always found it quite easy to do. So you should too!

THE HOLD

The ball is held between the heel of your strong foot and the shin of your weaker leg.

1. Start with your weak foot flat on the ground with the ball just in front of it.

2. Use your weaker hand and roll the ball up your weaker leg to halfway between your foot and knee.

3. Now place the heel of your stronger foot on the other side of the ball and press it into your shin.

To make sure you have the hold right, either hop around a bit to see if it drops out or you can try using your stronger heel to roll the ball up and down your shin.

THE TRICK
Step 1

Start with the ball in your hands at about waist height. Gently spin the ball up in the air so that it will bounce about 3–6 feet (1–2 m) in front of you with enough spin for it to bounce back and hit you in the shin.

Step 2

Move into position so the ball will hit
you in the shin of your weaker leg while
your weaker foot stays on the ground.

Tip

When you're learning this trick, don't
wear anything on your legs that will
make the ball slip off your shin, for
example, track pants or long soccer
socks.

Step 3

When the ball is about to hit your shin, quickly and smoothly bring your stronger heel up and press the ball into your shin.

Common Problem

I keep hitting the ball with the side of my stronger foot.

You're way too early with your stronger foot. You need to keep it out of the way till the ball is close to your weaker shin.

The Spinning Top

With this trick, you do a big jump and spin, and if you flick the ball out again quickly nobody really knows what you did, but they know it looked sensational!

THE HOLD

The ball is held between the back of your weaker calf and the inside of your stronger foot.

1 Bend over and use both hands to hold the ball against the back of your calf on your weaker leg.

2 Lift up your stronger foot and press the ball against your calf with the inside of your foot, then stand up straight.

To test you have the hold right, just hop around a bit. If the ball stays there, you've got it right.

THE TRICK
Step 1

As with the Shinny, gently spin the ball up in the air so that it'll bounce about 3–6 feet (1–2 m) in front of you with enough spin for it to bounce back and hit you at about shin height if you didn't move.

Step 2

While the ball is still in the air, spin around 180 degrees. Get into position so that the ball will hit the back of your calf on your weaker leg when it bounces back. Keep your eye on the ball all the time.

Tip

If the ball isn't going to land on your calf, jump at it. Some players actually find it easier to jump and catch the ball in one motion.

Step 3

When the ball hits the back of your calf, use the inside of your stronger foot to press and hold it there.

Variation

Don't spin at all but jump forward instead and catch the ball on the back of your weaker calf.

Common Problem

I catch the ball on the inside of my weaker leg or between my feet, not on the back of my calf.

This happens when you spin around too much, and to be honest I do this myself quite often. You've still caught the ball, so I wouldn't worry!

The Shoulder

I love to see a new trick and I can remember exactly when I first saw this one. It was done by Nakata, the Japanese soccer player.

THE HOLD

The ball is held between your shoulder and the side of your head. You lean a bit to the side so the ball is touching your head between your ear and your cheek.

1 Stand up straight and then tilt your upper body to the side a bit.

2 Place the ball between the side of your head and your shoulder.

3 Before you let go of the ball, swivel your head slightly so that you're looking upward.

Now go for a slow walk. If the ball stays where it is, you're ready to catch it there.

THE TRICK
Step 1

Start with the ball in your hands and throw it softly back toward you so that if you didn't move it would hit you smack bang on the end of your nose.

Step 2

When the ball is in the air, quickly turn 90 degrees so that the ball will now hit the side of your face.

Tip

Don't wear any clothing that will fill up the V shape you want the ball to fit into, such as a jacket with a big collar.

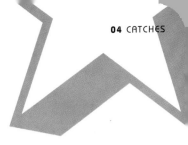

Step 3

Just as the ball is about to hit the side of your face, tilt your body away from the ball and it'll fall softly to rest in the hold you practiced earlier.

Common Problem

The ball always bounces about on my shoulder and then falls off.

If the ball hits your shoulder first, you're probably tilting your body away from the ball too early. If it hits your head first, either the throw is too high or you're tilting your body a bit too late.

The Thinker

I named this catch the Thinker after the famous Rodin statue.

THE HOLD

The ball is held between your thigh, your chest and your chin. It rests in the V shape between your thigh and your chest. Your chin is there just to stop it rolling off.

1 Stand up straight and hold the ball on your stronger thigh with your hand.

2 Lift your stronger knee up until the ball touches your chest.

3 Now rest your chin on the ball to keep it still.

If you can do a few hops without the ball falling out, you're doing everything right.

THE TRICK
Step 1

Start with the ball in your hands. Throw it straight up, but gently spin it back toward you.

Step 2

Lift your knee up as high as you can before you let the ball land on your thigh. Make sure your knee is higher than your hip so the ball rolls toward your chest.

Tip

Don't bring your chin down on a ball that's still bouncing or that isn't under control. You might bite your tongue or even lose some teeth. If the ball is still moving, lift your knee higher to get it to settle into your chest.

Step 3

When the ball touches your chest and has just about stopped moving, gently bend over and bring your chin down to rest on the ball.

Variation

Catch the ball on the end of your knee but don't use your chest or chin to hold it there, just lift your knee up to about the same height and the ball will balance on a spot just next to your kneecap.

Common Problem

The ball keeps rolling off over my knee before I can get my chin on it to stop it.

When you're bending over in Step 3, you're lowering your knee at the same time, so make sure when you bend your upper body that your knee doesn't move.

Juggling tricks

These tricks are what you learn how to freestyle for. These are the ones that look impossible, which just makes it even better when you do them in front of a crowd.

The Bounce Down

This is the first juggling trick I ever learned after I saw a display on TV by some Argentinean schoolboys during the World Cup in 1978.

Step 1

Kick the ball back toward yourself with your stronger foot so that it'll bounce between your feet.

Tip

If you can't juggle too well, start with the ball in your hands. Simply throw the ball gently down so it bounces between your feet and then do the Bounce Down.

Step 2

While it's still in the air, throw your stronger leg over the top of the ball.

Step 3

Just as the ball bounces, hop off your weaker foot. With the inside of that foot, tap the ball up and back in front to carry on juggling.

Variation

In Step 3, when the ball bounces, backheel it with your stronger foot onto the inside of your weaker foot to make it go upward.

Common Problem

I can do it, but the ball goes so far in front that I can't get to it.

You aren't kicking the ball back far enough in Step 1, so in Step 3 your weaker foot has to reach forward a long way. This results in the ball getting tapped forward, not upward.

The Drop

I thought I'd invented this trick until I saw an old training video where one of the players was doing it in the background while the coach was talking!

Step 1

Kick the ball with your stronger foot straight up to about head height.

Step 2

While the ball is in the air, twist your stronger leg so your knee is pointing down at the ground. Keep your stronger toes on the ground exactly on the spot where the ball will land and point your heel straight up in the air.

Tip

In Step 1, you have to be confident in yourself and kick the ball up to at least head height. You need to do this so it'll bounce high enough off your heel.

Step 3

Let the ball drop onto your heel. It'll bounce up into the air.

Variation

Lay the inside of your foot flat on the ground so the ball can bounce back up off the outside of your foot instead.

Common Problem

The ball always goes sideways off my heel.

If the ball goes behind you, you had some spin on the ball in Step 1. If the ball bounces the other way (toward you) you're leaning forward and your heel is angled too far over.

Helter Skelter

This is a unique trick because it uses the full length of your body and not many tricks go from head to feet.

Step 1

Head the ball straight up in the air.

Step 2

While the ball is still in the air, lift your stronger arm up and twist your upper body so that the ball will land on the back of your stronger shoulder.

Step 3

When the ball hits your shoulder, spin right around as quickly as you can. The ball will roll down across your back and land at your feet for you to carry on juggling.

Variation

Instead of heading the ball up in Step 1, start with the ball balanced on your forehead and then just let it roll off and do Steps 2 and 3.

Common Problem

I can never spin quickly enough to get the ball before it hits the ground.

Your problem is that you're spinning around too early, so the ball doesn't land on your back and roll, but just bounces off on its way down.

The Switch

I could never figure out how this trick was done until a few years ago, when a young boy did the Switch for me and I was able to see right away the mistake I'd been making!

Step 1

Hold the ball on your stronger foot and then lower your foot till your heel rests on the ground.

Step 2

Stand on your stronger heel and swing your weaker foot over the ball to the other side of it. Point your weaker toes right under the center of the ball.

Tip

Step 2 is a lot easier if you stick your bottom out a bit to balance yourself, and if you're really finding it tough to hold the ball, use a smaller one.

Step 3

Let go of the ball with your stronger foot and use your weaker foot to scoop up the ball and hold it.

Variation

Everything is the same but, instead of swinging your foot over the ball in Step 2, you just come alongside the ball and scoop it up with your weaker foot.

Common Problem

I can get the ball onto my weaker foot, but then I can't control it.

What's happening is that you're not scooping the ball up from underneath with your weaker foot. All you're doing is pushing the ball off your stronger foot.

The Scissor

I've seen this trick done by thousands of people and in some parts of the world it's called a Crossover.

Step 1

Kick the ball only slightly higher than normal with your stronger foot.

Common Problem

Every time I do it the ball goes off in front.

Usually it's because you're leaning back in Step 2, so when you hop you tend to kick the ball forward. Or your first kick in Step 1 might be forward.